TEST PIECE

SHERYDA WARRENER

COACH HOUSE BOOKS, TORONTO

first edition

Published with the generous assistance of the Canada Council for the Arts and the Ontario Arts Council. Coach House Books also acknowledges the support of the Government of Canada through the Canada Book Fund and the Government of Ontario through the Ontario Book Publishing Tax Credit.

LIBRARY AND ARCHIVES CANADA CATALOGUING IN PUBLICATION

Title: Test piece / Sheryda Warrener.
Names: Warrener, Sheryda, author.
Description: Poems.
Identifiers: Canadiana (print) 20220192642 | Canadiana (ebook) 20220192782 | ISBN 9781552454497 (softcover) | ISBN 9781770567382 (EPUB) | ISBN 9781770567399 (PDF)
Classification: LCC PS8645.A767 T47 2022 | DDC C811/.6—dc23

Test Piece is available as an ebook: ISBN 978 1 77056 738 2 (EPUB), 978 1 77056 739 9 (PDF)

Purchase of the print version of this book entitles you to a free digital copy. To claim your ebook of this title, please email sales@chbooks.com with proof of purchase. (Coach House Books reserves the right to terminate the free digital download offer at any time.)

for my friends

'The line marks, with infinite tenderness,
the experience of a body – a separate unknowable
experience inside the line, space outside it.'

– Anne Truitt, *Daybook*

'Most of our lives we live closed up in ourselves, with a
longing not to be alone, to include others in that life
that is invisible and intangible.

'To make it visible and tangible, we need light and
material, any material.'

– Anni Albers, 'Material as Metaphor'

TABLE OF CONTENTS

CRUSHED VELVET

Three women come toward me now up the city
block in matching citrus tones, crushed velvet.

On the off chance of catching a wayward spark,
I swerve into their path.

Lacking fluency, I fail to register.

Desire a material time turns outside in.

This is not the first time this trend has cycled
through in my lifetime.

Across temporary scaffolding, flowers whorl
on vines like sheets through dryer portals.

I drift in and out of propped shop doors, obey
the changeroom's sign by pulling the fine mesh bag
over my face to safeguard the garment from the
makeup I'm not wearing.

In the mirror, a sapling wrapped in burlap against
a wintry backdrop; when I remove the gauzey layer,
I've doubled in age and it's spring again.

At the apothecary, I let the consultant test samples.

Day's touchlessness reversed.

After rinsing me under lukewarm water, she makes a tidy
package with the towel, unwraps the gift of my own hand.

a *test piece* is an experimentation
with unconventional materials

A FIXED POINT

Stand in the colourless
plane face-to-face with the portrait,
taken by the unflinching features,

a spirit settled behind the eyes.
Mirror mechanism in the camera increases
the distance. No matter how long

I resist the brisk gallery pace,
it's the occasion of this glass façade
to hold subject separate

from viewer. The artist
stakes her claim, declares the original
a found object, makes a picture of

a picture. Here it hangs alongside
the artist's name, though *Alabama Tenant
Farmer Wife* remains nameless.

And yet the face retains a self-
possession even endless reproductions
– cut through by thick cables,

spliced by trivision – can't diminish.
Nothing disrupts that level stare. Determined,
I go out to meet her.

I go with my fraudulent,
matte-red mouth, thin-ribbed knit,
stand in her sightline, study

the natural composition – cotton floral
dress, hair's scattered part, lip bite, hardened
brow – try to locate a giving-

way. I'm the one who submits
in the end: imprecise, bound by the clock yet
frameless, inelegant, trying too hard.

I do as I'm told: try hard to conjure
a burning question, sip the coffee black, flip
the cup mouth-down, keeping

the question alive, hold to the count
of three, then another quick flick
upright. There in the interior's dark

the psychic reads what's forthcoming:
fine-grained, impeaching. I lie, say I can't
see it, even though I can.

I lie and say 'I see it,' even though
I can't, even as the reading stacks up: *How To
See, Art of Looking, Seeing Is Forgetting*

The Name of the Thing One Sees.
Tuck a folded paper under the back leg
to stabilize the table, set a raw silk

drop cloth to disguise the worn
exterior. The psychic says I'll come to
my senses, but I don't fully buy it.

Entering the gallery's rotunda,
a foil reflector shines upward, supported
by an assistant, illuminates

the railing, a woman in a red dress.
From my vantage point, her fiancé out of the frame,
I notice the sales tag before she tucks

it from sight. Who could afford
such a luxury, a mirror with no blind spots?
And what about the employee who,

after hours, wanted to take a closer
look and the Cryochamber door locked behind her?
My self-image flares up, then diminishes.

Register like a value in the unavoidable
bar mirror, part of the assemblage:
signature cocktail, sprig of wild

garnish, experimental florals, fractals
of conversations rising up from careless
impulsive speech, rounds of

recurring reactions, *ooh*s as steam
lets loose from baskets. A dislocated
voice bellows 'Is that the whole

fish?' as the server unwraps papillote
from around the silver flesh. Or, so I imagine –
my view obscured by a partition.

As if a partition lifts
and with it multiple divisions, this
primal tension works free

months later, sick in bed
streaming *Call Me By Your Name*,
right when from the layers of green —

Kodachrome, archival, olive,
seaweed, sea — the bronze sculpture
is dredged piece by piece:

chest plate, arms, head,
laurel braided into the hair, water emptying
through holes where eyes should be.

The discovery of a carved female figure
is considered invaluable not
by surviving eight thousand years

but by the rarity of its precise
wholeness. Is there such a thing? And can I
know it? All my revelations arrive

second-hand. As when in front of
the video install, a triptych of high-school kids
looking out, bright voices filling me in:

'the bottom half of her face is
a mirror' 'it looks like a T-shirt' 'something is
going to happen to her' 'it could be

inside emotions' 'the soul is going into
her mouth' 'that's how you would feel inside'
'in the face is all things – '

A BLUE FILTER

travelling southbound 8:17 a.m. express

> book in hand could be *Snow Country*
> or *Thousand Cranes*

blue flash in her periphery

> she looks up

from the train window
through late spring's foreign language

the book could be *The Sound of the Mountain* or
          The Old Capital

                    she looks up

gold and white stipples the blue

disruption to a green daily rhythm
                              dozy passengers fail to notice

        a door between compartments opens
                  generates a breezeway

Kawabata's voice over the loudspeaker

paper ads sway and clack
in the train's lurches

        she considers her own noticing a virtue

before it was an iris field it was an ordinary field of wild grasses, soil, weeds, etc., before the blue spears sensing light struck upwards broke the surface the woman didn't think to wonder what might have been growing there before she reads *irises prefer to be in close proximity to humans* before the paragraph when the iris motif appears on the girl's obi and later in a painting on the kitchen wall

memory stores in roots
reblooms

now she no longer recalls
shapes or colours, only

a sensation of irises

there/not there

even decades later
she recalls the field's noticing

slips in and out of
time, disrupts

takes shape from memory
passed down through
a blue filter

temporal ligature, triumphant motif
back-and-forthness

chorus of paper voices
in the zig-zag of time

8:17 a.m. train
appears / dissolves

she arranges her body iris-side
is met with a thresh-green line

in the middle of wild grasses a blue vibration

no –

it's the device buzzing
in the field of her hand

flowers cut, thrust into
buckets travel south in trucks
to be plucked at the market

later to spy periscopic
from alcoves, silhouettes against
translucent screens
dynamic arrangements

farmers gather at a picnic table
in communion with this flowerless edge

the woman on the train is impermanent as an iris
not the same going into the city as she is coming
home at night rush hour as buckets of irises spill
from buckets at market stalls she waits on the plat-
form to transfer trains a man in starched white
gloves approaches from behind shoves her body
into the compartment of anonymous bodies in the
lurch her face collides with a shoulder blade eyes
simultaneously close as the train travels under-
ground crush of impact lifts

                              a downy glove opens
                              in the field of her mind

what hands
what cramped

what airless what time
what time what hands what lurch
what cramped

as the train accelerates

flower/body retreat
into private stations

a ruthless blue-gold loop

she shunts out the doors
            into air   shoved up hard against

absence   even now her body stores the feeling

she does a little research
to find it

lifeless in a glass case at the gallery
decades later, another city (home)

dates back to the twelfth century
bleached cotton makes hands easier to see

what does a glove dream?

as she wanders tiltingly

from case to case

and on, into another room
a flattening

well after she leaves the exhibit

out-of-sequence fragments
proliferate even decades later

irises repeat
across various feeds: stained
glass, decorative paper, a blue burst
from a party cracker

one of three spring colourways

southbound across time

a train many trains clack and sway compartments empty and fill fields empty and fill buckets at markets empty and fill a man many men appear dissolve many gloves shove many trains clack and sway many hands fill memories in the body die down to the root rebloom

her body holds
the long blue sentence of it

she looks up

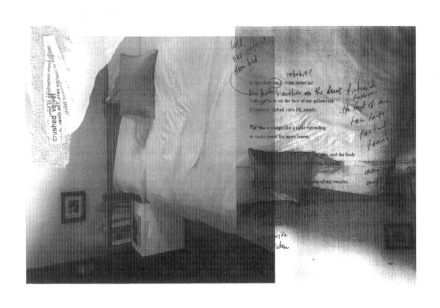

Is this the form it comes home to?

inhabit?

the body's outline on the sheet

Collects facts on the face of my pillowcase
Elsewhere, virtual ants fill, empty.

The dew unclasps like a table extending
to make room for more leaves.

... and the body

... arm of my sweater.

ON A CLEAR DAY

One minute I'm an empress laid out
on a marble slab, gold coins over my eyes, jewels

at my feet, and the next, my sleepmask slips as
an alarm disrupts and a hand lifts to silence –

Doubleness, and should I drift from? Day opens
like a curtain I shrug inside.

First: water, kettle, blue claw of flame,
three counter-clockwise turns to bloom the grinds.

Anemone's leafy fringe lifts my spirits.

Dollop of whip in coffee lifts my *esprit*.
A pint of blueberries in tiny crowns appoint me

ruler of this expanse. I crack the patio door for air.
Felted fish dolls stir above the sink. The artist

hid crystals in some and not others, not sure which
I have but here they hang at the hearth of all rituals.

A clear domestic space is a clear psychic space.

Before: email, class prep, *mamahaveyouseenmy???*–
I make my move.

a book planted
with colourful flags initiates a rhythm

     get a little contact high
          from language

          a jolt improves me

jumpstart
for the mind's engine

     stimulants appreciate
          in value

apply steadfast with clear senses

out from the centre

long horizontal bands alternate blue
alternate blue blue alternate light blue grey
silver light light blue

a set of gestures
opens the frequencies

Toaster pop signals the soft poach is ready
to be lifted from the roiling pot, a pouch

I could stuff all my things into, attach to a stick ...

Don't worry, I assure the succulents,
the seasoned cast iron. Above the table, a photo

of a space I once inhabited, a version of myself
recast back to me. Stuck between my own patterns,

this kitchen's grid of tiles – email, *brush your teeth,*
did you sunscreen, what if it IS what you mean –

repetition leads to fluency

a sheer weave
requires tending

                                        a pure
                                        concentration, no
                                        distraction

hold open a space
for the impulse to dip and flare

            where the threads shift   – careful! –
            a tendency to bruise

disturb the weave away from its woven uniformity

My son interrupts to ask if he can extend
his screen time. Dishes flourish in the sink,

the sheer height sets a new precedent. I make
my move, perform underwater sonatas

with the cutlery. Train my attention out beyond
the gingko and maple as an elderly terrier

is coddled up the street in the arms of its master.

What does she whimper in the dog's ear?
How earthly we behave, believing we're alone.

with a clear surface
and a little give

the mind thrives

catch in hand
a phrase or line then

pull taut

don't overwork it

A sticky note on the bay window: *fields of inquiry.*

Soften the dust cloth, cinch my sleepshirt
and Vanna around the apartment stimulating

with a light touch various neglected surfaces:
porcelain, wool, parquet. Joy the fixtures, freshen

the adages. Disturb with a circular motion
particulate matter before it accumulates.

Add to the list as I go: tub stopper, white vinegar,
all-over colour, flowers for Vi, *Art in Time.*

gestures of care
     and reparation

infinite forces

         a placement of intervals

           and the grid appears
           to waver

perceive in glimpses

    sleek as filament
confluence of threads

          shifts in precise increments

     disperse just as quick

Fish slip through the reeds of sentences,
crystals activate in caves. Broom rasp on pavement

as the neighbour sweeps the lot just out of sight.
Way back in the closet's dark, moths ruche holes

into cuffs and pockets of cardigans: late late
fragments. Turn the record, turn the clay pots, turn

toward the automated voice going by: YOU HAVE
REACHED YOUR ~~DESTINY~~ syllabus, text C & H

back, running from? – Plant blades impale air.

Backlit outsized shadows intensify, predatory.
Upstairs, chairs grind hard against

hardwood. The neighbour's voice amplifies,
making fun of his baby's cries.

From the patio, I banish detritus from the rugs.
Come back inside perfected with

bite marks, crescent shadows from the eclipse.
Everyday things mistaken for

everyday things: napkin swans, salami roses.

repetition a mode of
protection

        delicate calibration with a
           steady hand

a simple in-and-out flatweave
loosely woven

                nets the wild tacks

I use my powers to activate the fish – silver
now, gliding into the caulking

between tiles – smash them underfoot
in ashy heaps: unfinished elegies.

A clear domestic space is a clear psychic space!
Drag the seaweed of my hair from the drain.

Is there a poem here called 'Self'?
A comb missing three teeth.

Wipe the mirror clean with my face inside.

a constant negotiation
with real consequences

shrewd parameters

a rigid weave
encroaches

a hand loosely mends
the damages

Out walking, I have no real belongings.

My body invents a new cadence falling
in step with the sidewalk's incongruent lines as

my mind traffics in dreams: Time for a shrimp
cocktail? Spinach dip in a bread bowl?

An argument cuts through
leaf-shirred light: 'I want to make you happy

but don't know how,' and the park's self-cleaning
public toilet trips its own alarm.

alternate blue
alternate blue grey
alternate light light

Is this the form I come home to?

Cells are facts on the face of my pillowcase.
Bright chimes sound from another room, remote

as real fortune. Late afternoon unclasps,
a table pulled apart to make room for more leaves.

I miss the younger body within this one, and the
body within that one, and so on, take the misshapen

bean bag chair for my throne, tug off my bralette,
loosen myself within the structure.

I didn't make it to see *On a Clear Day*,
but when I turn from sink to photograph

yes, these infinite interiors coax life out of me.
When he wakes, my son will use the dark parts

to check if his hair is sticking up. Motifs appear
and re-appear, catching up with me: loud checks,

interlocking geometries, cast-off ends.
Now, what is it I'm looking for? In glass,

the open form assembles line by line.

Contact high is language.

I want to be audacious.

I want to wear wide-legged
crushed velvet pants & walk
down the sidewalk with my
friends. I want the occasion
for a spritzer, a dance party,
anything to raise

really know something of how
feels to see time pass. The sheer
1993, the pass. The sheer
pass. The sheet

what it feels like

TEST PIECE
after Eva Hesse

high up the gallery wall
a gold silk iridesces

gets me in the chest like   *gah!*
blindside

◆

                                   a shining structure
                                           that floats

                        I mean, it's this ridiculous form
                                 coming out of nothing

                         a moment yellow
                                      alive, as if

◆

Our host crushes diamonds of salt over olives in the
cast iron, adds them to the spread we gather
around. More friends arrive as the psychic brews
and pours the coffee, then moves around the circle
reading the grinds. Someone asks if there will be a
baby. Someone else asks about a promotion. The
future takes shape in the crux of our cups. What
does knowing do for us? And yet I want to know.

When she gets to me, she rotates counter-clockwise
from the handle, says I'll take a trip to the desert,
do I know what it is I'm looking for? I try to think
what might take me there as the face appears in the
sediment, and I can't tell if the features are buried
or exposed.

◆

the sculpture appears

     to lift lightly
on the air current in the atrium

as I lose my bearings

◆

it's so absurd
to have, out of that structure, this
little thing come out

here and here

a feeling of *oh*
of senses waking up

◆

Lunch at the artists' residency, a poet I admire asks
Can you say a little more about the poem? I attempt to

describe it. Eventually she turns to someone else.
On my way out of the dining hall, I steal the last
ground cherry from the dessert buffet, place the
husk to dry on the sill at the cabin. Handwashed
underwear hangs to dry on the patio railing,
weather arranges itself on invisible hooks. Cut-up
lines float on the flat top of the grand piano. Each
sharp point of the cabin's star juts out into forest.
On loan: *My Life* and a catalogue of textiles from
the collection at Stedelijk Museum in Amsterdam.
Out walking the Hoodoo trail my mind makes clean
loops: *can you say more / can you sail a little claim /
can you slake it / can you give a little / surface can you
salve / can you sooth-say / can you forsake it //* past
former versions of myself in quick succession, and
even then can't say for sure.

◆

close up   *oof*
in the chest again

not silk or silken or ephemeral but rigid
        sculpture's inner buoyancy
at various stages of decomposition
losing its sheen

        fraying here

and here

latex on cheesecloth
experimental artist-made resin

    a hoax

                  ◆

                              I am very real myself
                        with a nice patina and home

                        always a flower planted
                  on this body made of layers of

                          water, air, space, light,
                        skin and bones, terrain

                                  the open being

                  ◆

I appear in the grid for the ekphrasis workshop, a
copy of the readings beside me, fragment from
'Neither objects nor space, not time, not
anything – no forms' selected to share:

> in the drawings I love
> she leaves evidence
> of process fraying
> the grid's edge
> like leftover math

◆

The facilitator generates prompts, based on our selections. The one I offer:

Let the process show through, and fray.

And the one I receive:

Where the making of an image becomes an object in itself: activate that.

◆

inner buoyancy
I look around for a light source
skylight or clerestory

but it's coming from
inside

◆

a self isn't always self-evident

the face in the toilet mirror
could be anyone

look how it touches the glass

◆

I'm trying to describe how the poem hasn't yet
found its form when the mathematician holds out
her scarf, tells me she comes from a long line of
textile makers. 'You have to decide,' she says as she
flips the garment over in her hands, revealing the
weave's double logic, 'which side do you want to
hide, and which side do you want to face out?'

◆

'contingent' in the title
a combination of the French root
for 'to come together' and 'to touch'
'contingency plan' is a provision
for an unforeseen event or experience
'test piece' is a record of an experiment
with unconventional materials
materials are thought to be 'unconventional'
when it's unclear how they might behave or
transform under the duress of time

◆

the body is always softer
than its image

the body of a woman

a spectral text that survives
when all the language changes

infinite translations, infinite texts

such an intimacy
imagining an interiority

◆

Arriving early, I drink half a bottle of rosé while
waiting for Lindsay and Laura to show up, drop a
pin in the map so they know where to find me.
September, the warmth from the day trapped by
layers of smoke blown over from the interior.
Working up the nerve to swim, I change into my
suit without standing up, bring myself to the edge
and drop under, from a far way out look back,
marvel at this perspective. Soon they're on the
shore waving me in. We pour wine, toast to
friendship. It's not long before we've veered into
self-obsession versus intellectual posturing;
performance versus vulnerability; the audacity of
placing the self at the centre, can such a thing even
be done anymore? Confessions carry over into
direct messages the next day as we clarify our
positions. Laura circulates a photo of Linds and me
sinking down to our chins the instant the camera
comes out, heads bobbing on the surface – an
impulse we resolve in future to resist.

◆

outside the gallery, dancers
perform in the available window space
choreography in and out of sync
endless as a pure contour released
from the dream of the hand

◆

I hum in and out
and what does anything
make of me?

not the gingko or
the level gaze or
the speaking voice

just one more thing trying
to be a pattern in the world

◆

Cedar and I take a trip to the Similkameen to
celebrate my fortieth. She drives through the
shrub-steppes and screes as I read from *Human
Hours*, devolving into tears much of the time as I
work through something greater and more illegible
than I could name or know at the time. We take a
picnic to the lake where she experiments with
taking photos of me, but I complain that my eyes
are too puffy and she stops insisting. It's a long time
before I realize this is the desert the psychic saw in

the grinds. And later, back home, out walking the
nearby trails, listening to an interview with Hesse, the
self registers as such an imprecise form of
measurement, when really there are only these
earthen materials and what to make of them.

◆

circling the concourse
as monuments ancient and precise
cast shadows and water features carve
the present in high relief

      I come to with an urgency
      mutable gold force

◆

                time speeds up
                the appearance

            I no longer have a face
                  if I ever did

               and absurdity
               is the key word

NOTES

The photographic subjects of 'A Fixed Point' are *Alabama Tenant Farmer Wife,* 1936, by Walker Evans and *After Walker Evans,* 1981, by Sherrie Levine. The last poem in this sequence borrows language from the video installation *I See a Woman Crying (Weeping Woman),* 2009 by Rineke Dijkstra. I first encountered this work on exhibit at Bonniers Konsthall in Stockholm, Sweden, in 2011.

The flattened glove in 'A Blue Filter' refers to a Found MUJI object at *MashUp: The Birth of Modern Culture* at the Vancouver Art Gallery in 2016.

'On a Clear Day' borrows its title from a thirty-print suite of rectangular grids by Agnes Martin. This work, created following a period of inactivity, 'declares the long-sought-for clarity the artist had struggled to find in the barren New Mexican desert,' and returned her to painting and consistent work to the end of her life. *Art In Time* is by Cole Swensen. The question at the top of p. 60 is from *On Time* by Joanne Kyger.

'Test Piece' borrows its title from 'Test Piece for "Contingent," 1969' by Eva Hesse, living out its natural life at the National Gallery in D.C. The poem is an homage to the poets and artists who strengthen the root of my own brief time; their words make up the collage that appears on the right margin. In order of first appearance: Etel Adnan, Eva Hesse, Deborah Landau, Vija Celmins, Heather Christle, Dara Wier, Anne Truitt, Elizabeth Willis, Hannah Sullivan, Erín Moure, Kim Hyesoon, Elisa Gabbert, Kate Zambreno, Dorothea Lasky, Roo Borson, Renee Gladman, Mary Ruefle. The fragment on p. 68 is from *The Empty Form Goes All the Way to Heaven* by Brian Teare.

ACKNOWLEDGEMENTS

I'm grateful to everyone who contributed in some way to this collection over the years: my lovely family, friends, colleagues, and students.

Thank you to the editors who published earlier versions of poems: Cole Nowicki at fine. press; Naomi Sawada and Jay Pahre at the Morris and Helen Belkin Art Gallery. The Banff Centre provided space at a crucial time in the process.

Thank you to the folks at Coach House for their attention and care: Lindsay Yates, James Lindsay, Sasha Tate-Howarth, Tali Voron, Crystal Sikma, and Alana Wilcox. Special thanks to Crystal for transforming plain text into a beautiful material object.

Thank you to Amanda Wood for the stunning cyanotype, and for inspiring me with her practice. Thank you to Hoa Nguyen and Marina Roy for writing such generous accompaniments.

Thank you to Dorothea Lasky, Jennifer Nelson, Hoa Nguyen, and Silvina López Medin, whose workshops were essential to the thinking and making of these poems. Writing about Rosamunde Bordo's art led to my working in a collage mode; I'm grateful for the time spent with her work. Thanks also to Natalie Purschwitz for letting me live among her lively arrangements for a little while.

Thank you to Kim Nguyen and Bopha Chhay, for everything. Thanks to Psychic Cindy (Mochizuki) for the gift of her readings. Sandra Lo is also a kind of seer, and offered wise counsel over the years.

Thank you to Anne Simpson, who read an early draft of 'A Blue Filter.' Her notes and gentle nudges improved the writing immensely.

Love to Ian Williams, who asked vital questions, disrupting the poems just enough so that I could see myself in them more clearly.

Thank you to my beloved friends, whose conversation and correspondences directly influenced this work and made the poems possible: Claire Battershill, Cedar Bowers, Alison Braid, Lindsay Cuff, Heather Jessup, Keri Korteling, Angélique Lalonde, Laura Matwichuk, Emily Nilsen. It's a deep pleasure and a privilege to share in this pursuit of an artistic life.

I'm especially indebted to Laura for her impeccable taste in poems and art, and her unfailing belief in my work. And to Cedar, who sustains me with her brilliance and unconditional love.

Big hugs to my mom and my brother. And in loving memory of my dad. Finally, to Chris and Clyde, the great crushes of my life. You buoy me up!

Sheryda Warrener is the author of the poetry collections *Hard Feelings* (Snare, 2010) and *Floating is Everything* (Nightwood, 2015). Her work can be found in *Event, The Fiddlehead, Grain, Hazlitt,* and *The Believer,* among other literary journals. She is a recipient of *The Puritan*'s Thomas Morton Memorial Prize in Literary Excellence for poetry, and recent poems have been selected for *Best Canadian Poetry, The Next Wave: An Anthology of 21st Century Canadian Poetry,* and the 2020 CBC Poetry Prize longlist. Sheryda lives in Vancouver, BC with her son and partner, and teaches poetry and interdisciplinary forms in the School of Creative Writing at UBC.

Typeset in Arno and Scandia.

Printed at the Coach House on bpNichol Lane in Toronto, Ontario, on Zephyr Antique Laid paper, which was manufactured, acid-free, in Saint-Jérôme, Quebec, from second-growth forests. This book was printed with vegetable-based ink on a 1973 Heidelberg KORD offset litho press. Its pages were folded on a Baumfolder, gathered by hand, bound on a Sulby Auto-Minabinda, and trimmed on a Polar single-knife cutter.

Coach House is on the traditional territory of many nations, including the Mississaugas of the Credit, the Anishnabeg, the Chippewa, the Haudenosaunee, and the Wendat peoples, and is now home to many diverse First Nations, Inuit, and Métis peoples. We acknowledge that Toronto is covered by Treaty 13 with the Mississaugas of the Credit. We are grateful to live and work on this land.

Edited for the press by Ian Williams
Cover art *Untitled* by Amanda Wood
Cover and interior design by Crystal Sikma
Author photo by Jackie Dives

Coach House Books
80 bpNichol Lane
Toronto ON M5S 3J4
Canada

416 979 2217
800 367 6360

mail@chbooks.com
www.chbooks.com